We Gather Together

THE STORY OF THANKSGIVING

We gather together to ask the Lord's blessing;

He chastens and hastens his will to make known . . .

—Traditional hymn of thanksgiving,
Netherlands, 1625

HOME

We Gather

The STORY of

THANKSGIVING

ANKSGIVING

Together

RALPH and ADELIN LINTON

Henry Schuman · New York

Republished by Omnigraphics ● Penobscot Building ● Detroit ● 1990

Designed by Marshall Lee

*Currier & Ives illustration on title pages is used by
courtesy of the Mabel Brady Garvan Collection,
Yale University Art Gallery*

Library of Congress Cataloging-in-Publication Data

Linton, Ralph, 1893–1953.
    We gather together : the story of Thanksgiving / Ralph and Adelin
Linton.
        p.   cm.
    Reprint. Originally published: New York : Schuman,
c1949. Originally published in series: Great religious festivals
series.
    ISBN 1-55888-883-7 (alk. paper)
    1. Thanksgiving Day.   I. Linton, Adelin, 1899–   .   II. Title.
GT4975.L5   1990
394.2'683—dc20   89-43493
                                                                          CIP

∞ This book is printed on acid-free paper meeting the ANSI Z39.48 Standard. The infinity symbol that appears above indicates that the paper in this
book meets that standard.

Printed in the United States of America.

Contents

Illustrations

THE PUMPKIN

Ah! On Thanksgiving Day, when from East and from
    West
From North and from South come the pilgrim and
    guest,
When the gray-haired New England sees round his board
The old broken links of affection restored,
When the care-wearied man seeks his mother once more,
And the worn matron smiles where the girl smiled before,
What moistens the lip and what brightens the eye?
What calls back the past like the rich Pumpkin pie?

Oh—fruit loved of boyhood—the old days recalling,
When woodgrapes were purpling and brown nuts were
    falling!
When wild, ugly faces we carved in its skin,
Glaring out through the dark with a candle within!
When we laughed round the corn-heap, with hearts all
    in tune,
Our chair a broad pumpkin,—our lantern the moon,
Telling tales of a fairy who travelled like steam,
In a pumpkin-shell coach, with two rats for her team!

John Greenleaf Whittier

I

Over the River
and Through the Wood

THANKSGIVING is the oldest and most truly American of our national holidays. First celebrated by the Pilgrim Fathers and proclaimed anew each year by the President of the United States, it is as indigenous as the pumpkin pie which is the correct ending for every Thanksgiving feast. Moreover, it has changed less in its intention and in the manner of its celebration than any other of our holidays, national or international. The founders of America had never heard of most of the things we now do at Christmas or Easter, but Thanksgiving is still very much what the Pilgrims made it: a giving of thanks for Divine bounty coupled with a practical demonstration of that bounty. Churches of all denominations are open for services on this particular Thursday every year, but even the most devout divide attention between church and kitchen.

Quite as important as worship on this day is the renewal of family ties. Thanksgiving, even more than Christmas, is the holiday which brings scattered kindred together. The head of the family, or the member with the biggest house and the longest tablecloth, calls a gathering of the clan. Sons and daughters come with their spouses and children. Aunts and uncles from both sides of the family are drawn in. Small cousins eye each other shyly but by the end of the day, after the dinner, the games, and the cold-turkey sandwiches in the kitchen before leaving for home, they have become friends. Old family jokes and stories are shared and for a little while all hands bask in a sense of belonging to an intimate, affectionate group. They may go back to their separate homes later, but for a while they have been part of something larger than themselves.

Thanksgiving is also the time for sharing. It is hard to enjoy one's turkey if one knows that neighbors are hard put to it to get hamburger. The custom of providing Thanksgiving baskets for poor families is nearly as old as the holiday. Even our first Thanksgiving Day set a pattern for sharing, albeit more by accident than by intention. As will be narrated in Chapter V, the great Indian chief Massasoit, who had been invited by the Pilgrims to their feast, brought with him ninety braves with brave appetites. The hosts were startled but played up like men, although it cost them lean months the following winter.

Pilgrims and Indians, turkey and pumpkin pie are so much a part of the American tradition that it is hard for us to realize that the beginnings of Thanksgiving go back not only to the Old World but to the early world. The Pilgrims frowned on all the holidays of Merrie England and refused to celebrate even Christmas because they knew of its pagan origins. In proclaiming a day of thanksgiving after the crops were gathered and before winter set in, they may have taken a hint from the Old Testament, but they certainly did not know that they were acting in a tradition which went back to the time when men first began to sow and reap. Long before the dwellers by the Nile learned to measure the year or dreamed of building pyramids, all people who grew grain gave thanks at harvest time to the Beings who had given them their daily bread for the hard winter months. Moreover, these ancient farmers sensed in the changing seasons and in the cycle of seed-to-plant-to-seed again the miracle of death and resurrection and turned their wonder at it into legends.

II

Harvest Festivals of the Old World

THE Old Testament includes many references to harvest festivals. In the Book of Judges the Canaanites "went out into the field and gathered their vineyards, and trod the grapes and held festival, and went into the house of their god, and did eat and drink." In Deuteronomy it is recorded that Moses gave instructions to the Hebrews for the celebration of their harvest festival, which was called the Feast of the Tabernacles, because during this festival everyone lived in booths or tents in memory of the years when the children of Israel were wandering in search of the Promised Land. Said Moses: "Thou shalt keep the Feast of the Tabernacles seven days, after that thou hast gathered in from thy threshing floor and from thy wine press; and thou shalt rejoice in thy feast, thou, and thy son, and thy daughter, and thy manservant and thy maidservant, and the Levite and the stranger, and the fatherless, and the widow that are within thy gates. Seven days shalt thou keep a feast unto the

Lord thy God . . . because the Lord thy God shall bless thee in all thine increase and in all the work of thine hands, and thou shalt be altogether joyful."

In the Book of Nehemiah, the Lord commanded: "Go forth unto the mount and fetch olive branches, and branches of wild olive, and myrtle branches, and palm branches and branches of thick trees to make booths. . . . So the people went forth and brought them, and made themselves booths, every one upon the roof of his house, and in their courts, and in the courts of the House of God, and in the broad place of the water gate. . . . And there was very great gladness."

Even before Biblical times the ancient people of the Mediterranean basin held festivals at harvest time in honor of the Earth Mother. The Goddess of the Corn * was always one of the most important deities in the hierarchy of the gods, and her child was the young god of vegetation. Throughout mythology, this pattern is repeated: the Earth Mother and her child, the lovely youth whose nurses were Sunlight and Dew, who is sacrificed or abducted when the sere months of winter begin. When the young god has gone, the leaves fall from the trees and the grain sleeps underground; but when he is restored to his mother in the spring, the green shoots push up through

---

* "Corn" is the European term for any grain; Indian corn— our American "corn"—is called maize.

the brown earth and the land burgeons once again.

The ancient Semites called the Earth Mother Astarte and her symbol was the coiled serpent with the egg in its mouth, representing fertility. Her son was Tammuz, the young God of Vegetation. The Phrygians called her Semele, and her son was Dionysius. The Minoans had an Earth Mother for each district. All these local deities were absorbed by the Greeks into the one great goddess, Demeter, represented in white robes with sheaves of wheat and poppies in her hands. Her daughter Persephone was abducted by Pluto, the Lord of the Underworld. Because, during her sojourn in the nether kingdom, she ate some seeds of the pomegranate, she was doomed to spend part of the year with her grim lord. In the spring she returned to the upper world and the flowers bloomed and the young grain made the fields green again—the familiar parable of death and rebirth.

The most famous festival of Demeter was held in September at Eleusis. Only the initiated, the Mystae, could take part in the Eleusinian Mysteries, but these participants numbered several thousands and came from all parts of Greece. So important was the festival that even when the various Greek states were at war, as they frequently were, a general truce was held at this time. When the heralds went from town to town announcing the holding of the Mysteries, all hostilities were abandoned and the celebrants could make their journey to Eleusis in safety. They marched in procession, wearing garlands of myrtle and ivy and carrying sheaves of grain. The wealthy ladies of Athens, finding the four-hour march too wearisome, rode in their carriages, until the orator Lycurgus—who considered that this showed a lack of respect toward the goddess who had trudged for months seeking her abducted child—made it a law that no one could join the procession except on foot.

The public festival for Demeter, called the Thesmophoria, was held in October in a temple on the shore near Athens. Only married women participated in these rites. They went there, not in procession, but singly or in small groups under cover of night. Any male who inadvertently encountered any of the celebrants was subjected to mockery and mauling by the matrons; peals of feminine laughter would echo through the moonlit woods and bring others to join in the fun. Perhaps this custom was a device to keep prying male eyes away from the scenes of the rites, for the matrons spent the next day bathing nude in the sea and dancing and playing games on the shore. After these ceremonial sports, they returned to Athens where the festival continued for two more days. On the first day they fasted and sang dirges in memory of Demeter's sad pilgrimage, but on the second day there was feasting and singing and general gaiety and roistering, in celebration of the return of Persephone. Fruit and honeycombs

Ceres, or Demeter. From a Pompeiian wall painting

Ceres with two peasants. From a medieval miniature painting depicting sowing and reaping: He who plants the seed early shall reap the gold at the opportune hour (Courtesy of The Bettmann Archive)

were offered to the goddess and little pigs were sacrificed, in reprisal on the swine which had rooted in the growing grain.

The Roman harvest festival, held yearly in October, was called the Cerelia, after Ceres, the Roman goddess of the corn. This was a public festival with processions, music and dancing, rustic sports, and the feast, at which a sow and the first cuttings of the harvest were offered to the goddess.

With the acceptance of Christianity as the official religion of Rome and the conversion of the barbarians who had invaded the crumbling Empire, these pagan rituals were frowned upon and even forbidden by law. However, the peasants clung to them with a tenacity which has made the word "pagan" (originally meaning simply "villager") a synonym for "heathen." As late as the sixth century, when St. Benedict established the first monastery of his order at Monte Cassino, he found the local peasantry worshipping Apollo in a sacred grove. Even after conversion, old habits and beliefs died hard, and the Church was too busy trying to keep the flame of civilization alive to trouble with minor heresies.

The benevolent Earth Mother, purified of her grosser attributes and rites, blended with the equally benevolent Mother of Christ. Folk memory of local deities fused with the Christian tales of saints to provide patrons for villages, and the white-robed goddess of grain lived on in various guises. To those who live close to the soil, the harvest has an emotional and religious significance hard for dwellers in a modern city to understand. Its bounty means security against the bitter months to come and rest after toil. Their gratitude finds expression in rites in honor of the Being who they feel is most closely related to fruitfulness: a Being of warm earth rather than cold heaven.

Even today a half-pagan belief in the Corn Mother still survives among the peasants in many parts of Europe. Her spirit was thought to lodge in the last sheaf of grain left standing in the field, and various ceremonies were connected with its cutting. In some regions it was plaited and made into a doll which was dressed and decked with flowers and ribbons. This Corn Baby was carried home triumphantly and hung in the barn until the following harvest, insuring a good crop for the next year.

Sometimes the best ears of the last cutting were twined with flowers and made into a wreath which was worn by the prettiest girl in the village, or given to his sweetheart by the reaper who cut the last sheaf. She was fêted as the Corn Maiden, spirit of the harvest, Persephone returned to the upper world.

In Scotland and the north of Ireland, the last handful of corn to be cut was called the "kirn."

The reapers gathered around and each in turn threw his sickle at the last sheaf of standing grain. The one whose flying sickle cut the grain presented the sheaf to his sweetheart, who plaited and dressed it and made it into the "kirn doll." Another custom—somewhat reminiscent of the child's game of pinning the tail on the donkey— was for a reaper to be blindfolded and whirled around until he was dizzy, and then to try to cut the last sheaf while the others jeered and shouted at his wavering course and wildly swinging scythe. This game continued until one of the blindfolded reapers managed to cut the sheaf.

In eastern Europe, the reaper who cut the last sheaf of grain was hailed as the Corn Mother, dressed up in a gown made of sheaves of grain, and trundled through the village in a wheelbarrow, followed by laughing crowds.

The corn spirit was also believed to have various animal representations. In Slavic countries, when the ripening corn bowed and rippled in the wine, the peasant said that the Corn Dog was running through the field. In Austria, the Corn Cock was the spirit of the harvest. The last sheaf cut was called the Cocksheaf, and the reaper who cut it was the Cock of the Harvest. A live cock, or one made from pasteboard, painted and decked with ribbons, was mounted on the last load of grain. There was a grisly custom in Poland of burying the cock up to its neck in the corn field. The reapers would then swing at the bobbing, squawking head, and the first one whose scythe severed the head from the body was hailed as Cock of the Harvest.

III

The English Harvest Home

I<small>N</small> England special significance was attached to the last load of the grain brought home. The reapers and their friends and sweethearts, wearing garlands of flowers and ribbons, accompanied the load from field to barn, singing and making merry on the way. After this last load was safely stored, the Harvest Home supper was held. Robert Herrick's famous poem "The Hock-Cart" describes an occasion of this kind for seventeenth-century England:

THE HOCK-CART

or

Harvest-Home

Come, Sons of summer, by whose toil
We are the lords of wine and oil;
By whose tough labours and rough hands,
We rip up first, then reap our lands.
Crown'd with the ears of corn, now come,
And, to the pipe, sing Harvest Home!

We Gather Together

Come forth, my lord, and see the cart
Drest up with all the country art:—
See, here a maukin, there a sheet,
As spotless pure as it is sweet;
The horses, mares, and frisking fillies
Clad all in linen white as lilies:—
The harvest swains and wenches bound
For joy, to see the hock-cart crown'd.

About the cart hear how the rout
Of rural younglings raise the shout,
Pressing before, some coming after,
Those with a shout, and these with laughter.
Some bless the cart, some kiss the sheaves,
Some prank them up with oaken leaves;
Some cross the fill-horse, some with great
Devotion stroke the home-borne wheat;
While other rustics, less attent
To prayers than to merriment,
Run after with their breeches rent.
Well, on, brave boys, to your lord's hearth
Glitt'ring with fire, where, for your mirth,
You shall see first the large and chief
Foundation of your feast, fat beef!
With upper stories, mutton, veal,
And bacon, which makes full the meal;
With sev'ral dishes standing by,
As, here a custard, there a pie,
And here all-tempting frumenty.
And for to make the merry cheer,
If smirking wine be wanting here,
There's that, which drowns all care, stout beer;
Which freely drink to your lord's health,

The Story of Thanksgiving

Then to the plough, the commonwealth,
Next to your flails, your fanes, your vats;
Then to the maids with wheaten hats;
To the rough sickle, and crook't scythe,
Drink, frolick, boys, till all be blythe.
Feed and grow fat, and as ye eat,
Be mindful that the lab'ring neat,
As you, may have their fill of meat;
And know, besides, ye must revoke
The patient ox unto the yoke,
And all go back unto the plough
And harrow, though they're hanged up now
And, you must know, your lord's words true,
Feed him ye must, whose food fills you:
And that this pleasure is like rain,
Not sent ye for to drown your pain,
But for to make it spring again.

In Sussex the last load was called the Horkey cart and the harvest home feast was the Horkey. Robert Bloomfield's * poem "The Horkey" describes this feast:

Home came the jovial Horkey load,
    Last of the whole year's crop;
And Grace amongst the green boughs rode,
    Right plump upon the top.

Now Mrs. Cheerum's best lace cap
    Was mounted on her head;
Guests at the door began to rap
    And now the cloth was spread.

* English poet, 1766-1823. This poem was based on nostalgic memories of his boyhood on a farm in Suffolk.

And Farmer Cheerum went, good man,
   And broach'd the Horkey beer,
And sitch a mort of folks began
   To eat up our good cheer.

Sayd he, "Thank God for what's before us;
   That thus we meet agen",
The mingling voices like a chorus
   Join'd cheerfully Amen.

Welcome and plenty, there they found 'em—
   The ribs of beef grew light,
And puddings—til the boys go round 'em—
   And then they vanish'd quite.

Now all the guests, with Farmer Crouder,
   Began to prate of corn,
And we found out they talk'd the louder
   The oftener pass'd the Horn.

Out came the nuts; we set a cracking;
   The ale came round our way
By gom, we women fell a clacking
   As loud again as they.

John sung "Old Benbow" loud and strong,
   And I "The Constant Swain".
"Cheer up, my Lads" was Simon's song
   "We'll conquer them again".

And twelve o'clock was drawing nigh
   And all in merry cue;
I knocked the cask, "Oho", said I,
   "We've almost conquer'd you".

34

My Lord begged round and held his hat,
  Says Farmer Gruff says he,
"There's many a Lord, Sam, I know that,
  Has begged as well as thee".

Bump in his hat the shillings tumbl'd
  All round among the folks;
"Laugh if you will", said Sam, and mumbled,
  "You pay for all your jokes".

These last verses refer to the custom of passing the harvest cheer as each man sang a song, and the Lord was the reaper who cut the last grain and was privileged to be lord of the harvest and collect his fees from all the guests.

A similar Harvest Home supper for England in the early nineteenth century is described in Chapter 53 of George Eliot's *Adam Bede*. "As Adam was going homewards . . . he saw in the distance the last load of barley winding its way toward the yard gate of the Hall Farm, and heard the chant of 'Harvest Home' rising and sinking like a wave. The work he had to do at home, besides putting on his best clothes, made it seven before he was on his way again to the Hall Farm, and it was questionable whether, with his longest and quickest strides, he should be there in time even for the roast beef, which came after the plum pudding, for Mrs. Poyser's supper would be punctual.

"Great was the clatter of knives and pewter

plates and tin cans when Adam entered the house.
. . . It was a goodly sight—that table with Martin Poyser's round good-humoured face at the head of it, helping his servants to the fragrant roast-beef and pleased when the empty plates came again. Martin, though usually blessed with a good appetite, really forgot to finish his own beef tonight—it was so pleasant to him to look on in the intervals of carving and see how the others enjoyed their supper; for were they not men who, on all the days of the year except Christmas and Sundays ate their cold dinner, in a makeshift manner under the hedgerows and drank their beer out of wooden bottles. . . . Martin Poyser had some faint conception of the flavour such men must find in hot roast-beef and fresh-drawn ale. . . . But now the roast-beef was finished, and the cloth drawn, leaving a fair deal table for the bright drinking cans and the foaming brown jugs and the bright brass candlesticks, pleasant to behold. Now the great ceremony of the evening was to begin—the harvest song in which every man must join. He might be in tune, if he like to be singular, but he must not sit with closed lips. The movement was obliged to be in triple time; the rest was *ad libitum*."

Harvest festival in Poland, showing the Cock of the Harvest
(Courtesy of The Bettmann Archive)

Harvest-Home at Hawkesbury on Cotswold.

The last in-gathering of the crop
Is loaded, and they climb the top,
And there huzza with all their force,
While Ceres mounts the foremost horse :
" Gee-up!" the rustic goddess cries,
And shouts more long and loud arise ;
The swagging cart, with motion slow,
Reels careless on, and off they go!

The English Harvest Home

THE LANDING
OF THE PILGRIM FATHERS

The breaking waves dashed high
  On a stern and rock-bound coast,
And the woods, against a stormy sky,
  Their giant branches tossed;

And the heavy night hung dark
  The hills and waters o'er,
When a band of exiles moored their bark
  On the wild New England shore.

Not as the conqueror comes,
  They, the true-hearted, came,
Not with the roll of stirring drums,
  And the trumpet that sings of fame;

Not as the flying come,
  In silence and in fear,—
They shook the depths of the desert's gloom
  With their hymns of lofty cheer.

Amidst the storm they sang,
  And the stars heard and the sea!
And the sounding aisles of the dim wood rang
  To the anthems of the free!

The ocean-eagle soared
From his nest by the white waves' foam,
And the rocking pines of the forest roared,—
This was their welcome home!

There were men with hoary hair
Amidst that pilgrim-band;
Why had *they* come to wither there,
Away from their childhood's land?

There was woman's fearless eye,
Lit by her deep love's truth;
There was manhood's brow serenely high,
And the fiery heart of youth.

What sought they thus afar?
Bright jewels of the mine?
The wealth of seas, the spoils of war?—
They sought a faith's pure shrine!

Ay, call it holy ground,
The soil where first they trod!
They have left unstained what there they found—
Freedom to worship God.

Felicia Dorothea Hemans

IV

Squanto—
a Neglected Hero

T<small>HE</small> Pilgrims undoubtedly brought memories of such English Harvest
Home celebrations with them when they came to
the New World. They had also witnessed "thanksgiving" ceremonies during their sojourn in Hol-
land, for the Dutch were addicted to proclaiming public days of prayer and thanksgiving to com-
memorate military victories and other special
events. The Pilgrims themselves would have denied that the thanksgiving feast in honor of their
first harvest in 1621 was evoked by memories of
the profane practices of the Old World; however,
all revolutionaries, political or religious, once
their goal is accomplished, turn back to the pat-
terns of the society in which they have been reared,
and the Pilgrims, at the time of the first Thanksgiving, were no exception.

To be sure, the Pilgrims felt that human ceremonies should respond to the dispensations of
Providence and they objected to celebrations fixed
by the calendar. It was not until 1863, 242 years

after the Pilgrim harvest feast, that Thanksgiving became an annual event, and even now the date is supposedly announced each year and not fixed by the calendar, which may be a concession to the Pilgrim attitude. The holidays of the Church of England were regarded by the Pilgrims as "Roman corruptions." There was no warrant in Scripture for Christmas or Easter and only the most benighted would take cognizance of such pagan rituals.

On their first Christmas in Plymouth, the colonists worked hard laying out the site of their Common House and felling timbers. The skipper of the *Mayflower*, who didn't share the Pilgrims' scorn for this day, broke out a barrel of beer and drank Christmas toasts with his crew. Some of those still living aboard the ship joined in, but for the weary men ashore there were only scant rations and little shelter against the "sore storme of wind and raine" which battered the coast that Christmas night.

The harvest feast of the following autumn was the first holiday which the colonists had recognized in their new home. They were in a mood for rejoicing. The specter of starvation no longer menaced (or so they thought); they were at peace with the Indians; and they rejoiced to be able to share their bounty with the savages and to let their weary spirits soar in three days of feast and sport with scant emphasis on religion.

The man whose help and devotion contributed most to making that autumn a time of thankfulness rather than despair was a Patuxet Indian—Squanto, or Tisquantum. Squanto has never received his due from American history. Though New England is dotted with monuments and plaques immortalizing the names of the Pilgrim fathers, there is no formal tribute to the Indian Saint of Plymouth. Only a lonely promontory on the Massachusetts coast, Squantum Point above Quincy, and a grubby side street in Plymouth are named for him.

From the beginning, Squanto's destiny was strangely linked with that of the white men. In 1605, an English exploring party led by Captain George Weymouth had landed on the coast of New England in the region later settled by the Pilgrims. In the course of their explorations they captured several Indians whom they took back to England with them as souvenirs of the voyage. Among these was Squanto, a young brave of the Patuxet. Squanto was apparently well treated in England (there is little information about this first adventure among the whites), but he pined for his native land.

In 1614, when Captain John Smith set out on an expedition to the New World, Squanto sailed with him. The fleet landed at Plymouth (then called Thieves' Harbor), and Squanto returned to his tribe, though not for long. One of the ships in Smith's fleet remained in the New World when the other sailed. Its commander, Captain Thomas Hunt, was instructed to trade with the Indians and collect a cargo of beaver pelts and fish. In the course of this trading, Hunt, a dishonest rascal, lured some Indians aboard his ship, where he had them bound and thrown into the hold. Among these unfortunates was the recently returned Squanto.

Hunt sailed for Spain, where he put into the port of Malaga and sold the "poor silly salvages for rials of eight" in the slave market there. The other Indians were never heard of again. They probably died rather than submit to white domination, for the red men were never broken to slavery. Squanto, however, had the good fortune to be bought by some local friars who treated him well and gave him instruction in the Christian faith. Some years later he managed to get away to England, where John Slanie, treasurer of the Newfoundland Company, discovered him and took him into his home.

But again Squanto yearned for his own home. When Mr. Slanie learned that his friend Captain Thomas Dermer was setting forth on an exploring trip to New England, he made arrangements for Squanto to go along. In 1619, Squanto arrived once again on his native soil—probably the first American Indian to make two round trips to Europe.

Captain Dermer's first port was the Island of Monhegan off the coast of what is now called

Maine. This island was an important English fishing station in those days. Here the vessel picked up Samoset, a chief of the Wabenake. They then sailed for Plymouth Harbor, dropping anchor there about six months before the arrival of the Pilgrims.

This was the territory of the Patuxet. But Squanto, eager to rejoin his own people once more, found only loneliness and horror. While he had been in England a plague had exterminated the entire tribe; all his family, all his tribesmen, were gone. He found only empty fields and deserted villages, in some of which the dead still lay unburied in the crumbling huts. This plague was probably either smallpox or measles. These diseases were unknown on the American continent until they were introduced by the European sailors, and to the aboriginal population, who had built up no immunity to them, they were as deadly as the Black Death.

After his tragic homecoming, Squanto went to live among the Wampanoag, a neighboring tribe, who had also been sadly decimated by disease. But they were not his people and Squanto was restless and unhappy.

The Indians, having good reason to be suspicious of the whites, had kept their distance for some time after the colonists' arrival. The Pilgrims during their first few months in the New World had seen only small parties of Indians in the distance.

Samoset, Squanto's friend, the Wabenake from Monhegan, made the first overture toward the white men. About the middle of March, Samoset, escorted by a small band of Wampanoag, entered the Plymouth territory. The other Indians remained in the woods on the far side of the stream, but Samoset marched confidently down the main street of the little village, to the astonishment and consternation of the colonists. William Bradford reported that "he very boldly came all alone and along the houses stright to the Randevous, where we intercepted him, not suffering him to goe in, as undoubtedly he would out of his boldness. He saluted us in English, and bad us well-come for he had learned some broken English among the Englishmen that came to fish at Monchiggon and knew by name most of the Captaines, Commanders & Masters." He was the first savage with whom the Pilgrims had spoken and they were amazed to find him self-possessed and friendly.

His costume, or rather lack of it, embarrassed the modest colonists, for he was "stark naked, onely a leather about his wast, with a fringe about a span long." They hurriedly wrapped him in the cloak of one of the elders on the pretext that the wind was rising, but it is more likely that they were protecting their womenfolk from the spectacle of a naked man.

Samoset stayed several days; in fact, he enjoyed the hospitality so much that the colonists had to drive him away, for they could not continue to entertain him with white bread and "strong waters" from their meager stores. He returned a week later, however, bringing Massasoit (Sagamore of the Wampanoag), his brother Quadquena, sixty of their men—and Squanto.

This was a Thursday, the 22nd of March, "a very fayre, warm day." The other Indians departed after they had received suitable hospitality, all except Squanto, who adopted the Pilgrims as his own people and never left them until his death two years later.

Squanto, already a Christian when he joined the colony, became one of the Pilgrim Saints, as those were called who held to the strictest tenets of the Pilgrim theology; the colonists who were more lax in doctrine were known as Strangers. Squanto's gifts as an interpreter, his understanding of the habits and attitudes of the Indians, his knowledge of the techniques of hunting, fishing, and farming in that environment, all were invaluable to the colonists. It was largely due to Squanto that the Pilgrims were able to establish and preserve peace and friendly trade with their aboriginal neighbors. Governor Bradford records that he was "a special instrument sent by God for their good beyond expectation." He endeared himself the second day he was with them by going "at noon to fish for Eeles, at night he came home with as many as he could well lift in one hand, which our people were glad of, they were fat & sweet, he trod them out with his feete, and so caught them with his hands without any other instrument."

The devout band which had landed on Plymouth Rock in December 1620 were a courageous and hardworking lot, but they were ill-equipped, both personally and materially, for hewing a livelihood from a formidable wilderness. They were for the most part townsfolk, shopkeepers, and artisans, and few of them had had experience in farming or building. They had not even brought adequate tools for cutting timber, or lines and hooks for fishing. They had been drawn to the New World, not by the lure of new lands to exploit, but by their zeal for serving the Lord in their own way, and they expected Him to give them strength. It does seem that some Divine Providence was looking after these innocents, for despite all their hardships they did manage to survive and to found a permanent colony, which would have been impossible if certain fortunate circumstances had not combined to aid them.

The extermination of the Patuxet, while tragic for the tribe, was not an ill wind which bore nobody good. If the Pilgrims had landed in the territory of a strong tribe who jealously guarded their cleared fields and their hunting grounds, the band could never have established a foothold on these shores. They barely survived that first winter, even when they were able to take over the

Patuxet lands with no interference from the Indians.

The arrival of Squanto was another great blessing, for without his help they would have had no corn crop to be thankful for that autumn and they could not have established peaceful trade relations with the Indians.

The third piece of good fortune was the finding of a cache of Indian corn. The Pilgrims probably considered this to be an act of Providence also, although the aborigine who had raised and stored the corn must have regarded it as plain larceny. This happy find occurred shortly after the *Mayflower* had made its first landing at Cape Cod, in what is now Provincetown Harbor. Here on November 13th, 1620, the weary voyagers who had been shut up in the storm-tossed little ship for over two months at last felt solid ground under their feet.

The children, wild with joy, ran shouting up and down the beaches. The women brought out great bundles of dirty clothes and did a gigantic laundering in the fresh streams—a service "of which they had great need," as can well be imagined. Ravenous for fresh food, the young people waded into the chill waters and dragged out oysters, mussels, and crabs, which were gobbled by all the voyagers, with dire results in some cases. During all this activity the sentries kept an anxious watch, for none knew when savages might come swooping over the dunes.

Captain Miles Standish organized a scouting party to explore the territory to see whether or not it was desirable for settlement. In spite of the fine harbor and the prepared fields, they determined to look farther, for there was not an adequate supply of fresh water on the sandy Cape.

The explorers encountered only one small party of Indians, who fled at sight of them. However, they saw harvested corn fields, Indian huts, and a number of graves, which they dug up but restored again because they felt it would be "odious unto us to ransacke their Sepulchers." The houses were round "like unto an Arbour" and made from sapling branches covered with mats, with a chimney hole in the top. The huts had been recently vacated, for the white men found there fresh venison, earthenware pots, and baskets made from crab shells and from woven fiber. They calmly helped themselves to "some of the best things."

Their most important discovery was made near what is now the village of Truro at the spot still called Corn Hill, which was the Pilgrims' name for it. Here hidden under hillocks of sand they found a large woven basket containing about four bushels of seed corn, which had been cached there by the natives for spring planting—"some 36 goodly eares of corne, some yellow, and some red, and others mixed with blew, which was a very goodly sight." (Maize, or Indian corn, is an American plant that was unknown in Europe until the early explorers began to take it back home with them.) There was more in the cache than the marauders could carry, but they filled an iron kettle which they had with them, stowed as much as they could about their persons, and made careful note of the location.

A few days later they returned and got the rest of it, as well as several other caches which they discovered, making about ten bushels in all. "And sure it was God's good providence that we found this Corne, for els we know not how we should have done, for we knew not how we should find, or meete with any of the Indians, except it be to doe us a mischiefe." It apparently never entered their pious heads that they were doing a "mischiefe" in depriving the poor savages of their next year's crop. It is fortunate that the Pilgrims decided to move on to Plymouth, for they would scarcely have been popular in that territory and they could not have taken over the corn fields without a bitter fight.

These stores of seed corn would not have been enough to save the colonists from starvation the next winter if they had not had the vacant corn fields of the Patuxet in which to plant the crop. The labor of clearing fields and building houses in one winter would have been more than they could do. Nor would the fields have been enough if they had not had Squanto to teach them how to handle the crop. The Patuxet lands were old, exhausted fields which would not produce without fertilization. Squanto showed them how to plant the corn

in properly spaced hillocks with three little herring in each hill, their noses together and their
tails fanning out. He also helped them to build
weirs in the brooks to catch the herring at the time
of the spring run and cautioned them to put guards
over the fields to prevent the ravenous animals
from digging up the fish. The time for planting
corn, Squanto said, was when the leaves of the oak
tree were the size of a squirrel's ear.

The Pilgrims had much to be thankful for that
first autumn in the New World. They had survived their first terrible winter; that is, a sufficient number had survived so that the colony could
be carried on. Of the hundred who had landed
from the *Mayflower*, only fifty survived to participate in the first Thanksgiving feast. Half of
the original colonists lay under unmarked, plowed-
over graves; the colonists had not dared to hold
funeral services or to mark the graves, not wishing to let the savages know how many of their
number were gone. In many cases whole families
had been wiped out, and only one had not lost at
least one member. This was the Billingtons, who
were not among the "Saints," being considered
quite "prophane" by the more orthodox members
of the group. That this family should have survived intact while the more godly perished must
have given the Saints to ponder on the inscrutable
ways of the Lord.

The death toll was highest among the women;

only five out of eighteen wives survived. The women probably denied themselves their share of the rations—already down to starvation level during that winter—in order that their children might have enough food. There were some days during January and February when only a handful of men were well enough to go forward with the urgent tasks. The many deaths were not due to any epidemic. From the inadequate records we have, they seem to have been due to a combination of scurvy (there was little to eat except bread made from the meal brought by the *Mayflower*) and pneumonia caused by exposure and weakened physical condition.

But with the coming of spring there were wild greens which could be eaten as "sallet"; there were berries and fruits; and the fish and game became plentiful enough so that even such inept fishermen and hunters as the Pilgrims could bag all that they needed. With the warm weather and a balanced diet, the health of the colonists improved. Governor John Carver died of a sunstroke that spring from working in the fields without a hat; but after this sad loss there were no deaths and little sickness all that summer. When the *Mayflower* sailed for England, not a single colonist elected to turn from the rigorous life in the New World and go back with the ship.

The Pilgrims could face the coming winter in the knowledge that they would have adequate shelter. There were eleven houses along the village street that autumn, seven private dwellings and four community buildings. This was hardly luxurious quarters for fifty persons; but to many of the company, who had been forced to live aboard the *Mayflower* until the 21st of March, four months after they had first set foot on land, to have a home of any kind on solid ground was a great joy. Housebuilding was a laborious process, for they were not experienced carpenters and had only the most essential of tools. Their houses were not "log cabins," it must be remembered. The log cabin, which we are accustomed to thinking of as standard wilderness architecture, was unknown in the New World until the Swedes and Finns who settled along the Delaware brought the pattern with them. The Pilgrims struggled along with houses of wattle-and-daub with steep thatched roofs like those they had known in England.

The colonists had cause for thanksgiving in that they had established friendly relations with their savage neighbors and could "walk as peaceably and safely in the woods as in the highways of England." That spring shortly before Governor Carver's death, the colonists made a formal treaty of peace with Massasoit. The first arrangements were made with Squanto as go-between.

Massasoit, his brother Quadquena, and a large company of braves arrived on the appointed day but halted on a hill on the other side of the brook from the Pilgrim settlement. They demanded that an envoy be sent to them. Edward Winslow was selected, as a courageous and diplomatic young man. Winslow presented to the Sagamore the greetings of his governor and also of King James of England. This made less impression than the gifts of jewelry, knives, biscuits and butter, and "firewater" which Winslow had also brought.

Leaving Winslow as a hostage with the red men on the hill, Massasoit and a small escort crossed the brook and proceeded to the house where the parley was to take place. Behind him marched Miles Standish and his company of eighteen soldiers in full regalia with trumpet and drum sounding the martial note, a tribute which caused Massasoit to tremble with terror.

Bradford recorded the following description of Massasoit at this parley: "In his person he was a very lusty man, in his best years, an able body, grave of countenance, and spare of speech; in his attire little or nothing differing from the rest of his followers, only in a great chain of white bone beads about his neck, and at it behind his neck hangs a little bag of tobacco. His face was painted a sad red like murrey, and oiled, both head and face, that it looked greasily."

With Squanto and Samoset as interpreters, Governor Carver and Massasoit worked out the terms of the treaty as follows:

"1. That neyther he [Massasoit] nor any of his should injure or doe hurt to any of our people.

"2. And if any of his did hurt to any of ours, he should send the offender that we might punish him.

"3. That if any of our Tooles were taken away when our people were at worke, he should cause them to be restored, and if ours did any harme to any of his, wee should doe the like to them.

"4. If any did unjustly warre against him, we would ayde him; if any did warre against us, he should ayde us.

"5. He should send to his neighbour Confederates, to certifie them of this, that they might not wrong us, but might be likewise comprised in the conditions of Peace.

"6. That when their men came to us, they should leave their Bowes and Arrows behind them, as wee should doe our Peeces when we came to them."

Though this was an oral treaty, with puffs upon Massasoit's peace pipe taking the place of seals and signatures, it stands as one of the most successful nonagression pacts in history, wrought by a handful of white men with one of the most powerful chieftains of New England. Bradford, in recording these events twenty-four years later, said that this treaty had never been broken.

V

The First
Thanksgiving

ALL in all, in spite of the many hidden graves, the Pilgrims had cause for rejoicing that autumn and were in a mood for a real holiday, the first in the grim year. After months of semistarvation rations, they now felt that they could afford to spread themselves and give a true harvest feast. The weekly ration— one peck of meal per person from the stores of the *Mayflower*—was now increased by one peck of corn per week per person. Game, fish, and fruits were plentiful in the autumn season.

Edward Winslow wrote an account of the harvest feast in a letter sent back to a friend in England: "Our corne did prouve well and God be praysed we had a good increase of Indian corne, and our Barly indifferent good, but our Pease not worth the gathering. . . . Our harvest being gotten in, our Governor [William Bradford] sent foure men on fowling that so we might after a more speciall manner rejoice together, after we had gathered the fruit of our labours; they foure in one day killed as much fowle, as with little helpe beside served the Company almost a weeke, at which time amongst other Recreations, we exercised our Armes, many of the Indians coming amongst us, and among the rest their greatest King Massasoit, with some ninetie men whom for three days we entertained and feasted and they went out and killed five Deere, which they brought to the Plantation and bestowed on our Governour, and upon the Captain Miles [Standish] and others. And although it be not alwayes so plentifull, as it was at this time with us, yet by the goodnesse of God, we are so farre from want that we often wish you partakers of our plentie."

Squanto was dispatched to invite Massasoit to join the thanksgiving feast, and it was expected that he would bring his brother and a small company of braves. When, as we have seen, he turned up with ninety men—thereby outnumbering the hosts by forty (there were only fifty adults and five children)—the colonists were unquestionably taken aback.

A harvest feast was not a new idea to the Indians. All the tribes along the eastern seaboard celebrated the ripening of the harvest with a ritual called the Green Corn Dance. Just what form this took among the Wampanoag we do not know, since the Pilgrims—even if they were aware of their neighbors' pagan festivals—would have

German harvest festival

" Home came the jovial *Horkey load*,
" Last of the whole year's crop ;
" And Grace amongst the green boughs rode
" Right plump upon the top.

The Horkey load. Illustration by George Cruikshank

*Statue of Massasoit in Plymouth, Massachusetts
(Courtesy of the Pilgrim Society)*

*The first Thanksgiving dinner in New England. From an old
print. Actually, the Pilgrims did not build log cabins, as is
noted in the text, nor did the east coast Indians of the period
wear fringed shirts*

scorned to include such heathen corruptions in their reports.

We have early accounts of the Green Corn Dance among the Cherokees of the Southeast. The Busk, as they called it, lasted for four days, with rites of purification during which the whole village was cleansed and renewed, all old clothes and old provisions were discarded, new fires were kindled, and the year began afresh with the feasting on the new corn.

The Wampanoag turned out ninety strong—in the belief, no doubt, that they had been invited to join in the Pilgrim version of the Green Corn Dance. It was their aboriginal high spirits that contributed largely toward breaking the pattern of Pilgrim severity and making the first Thanksgiving a time of prolonged feasting and revelry. Since the Indians, like most primitive people, have the happy capacity for gorging as long as food is available, then subsisting comfortably on the surplus until the next meal turns up, we can be sure that the guests stowed away enough provender for a week during the three days at Plymouth.

In addition to the five deer contributed by the Indians, the menu included turkeys, wild geese and ducks, lobsters, eels, clams, oysters, and fish. The wild fruits of the summer: gooseberries, strawberries, plums and cherries, had been dried, a practice the Pilgrims learned from the Indians, for there was no sugar for making the customary jams or jellies. The nearby bogs abounded in cranberries, which the Pilgrims may have gathered and dried as the Indians did, though there is no mention of the bitter red berries which now grace every Thanksgiving table. The colonists certainly hadn't sugar enough for cranberry sauce. There is a very early New England recipe for a steamed pudding made from chopped cranberries, flour, and molasses, which the Pilgrims may have made. They also probably cooked some of their dried fruits in dough cases, the forerunner of the famous New England pies.

Pumpkin pie was certainly not on the menu that October. Though the Indians raised some pumpkins and may have offered a few to their neighbors, it is doubtful that the pilgrims knew what to do with this formidable vegetable. The later colonists used it extensively (they called it "pompion") as sauce and in bread as well as pie. One early rhymester wrote:

"We have pumpkins at morning and pumpkins at noon,
If it were not for pumpkins, we should be undone."

And an old colonial drinking song begins:

"Oh, we can make liquor to sweeten our lips,
Of pumpkins, of parsnips, of walnut tree chips."

The Pilgrims were not so experimental in their brewing, but they sweetened their lips at the first Thanksgiving with wine made from the grapes, white and red, which grew in profusion in the New

England countryside. Their first vintage must have been somewhat green that October, but it was brought out by the gallon for the feast, supplemented (and perhaps spiked) with the "strong waters" from their English stores.

There were biscuits and bread of English wheat, and corn in various forms: parched corn, roasted corn, hoe cakes and ash cakes, and Indian pudding made of cornmeal and molasses boiled in a bag. All these were Indian dishes which Squanto had taught the colonists to prepare. It is quite possible that the Pilgrim children munched happily on popcorn balls, for though there is no mention of this confection we know that the Indians of the region used popcorn long before the coming of the whites. They shook it over the coals in earthen jars and then poured maple syrup over it and made it into sticky balls. Think of the amazement and delight of the first white children who watched the dry kernels burst into fluffy whiteness!

Cooking was done largely in the open, with venison and turkeys and geese turning on the spits, lobsters and oysters roasting in the coals, and clam chowder and venison stew simmering in iron kettles over the fire. One can imagine the weariness of the women during those festive three days. There were only five matrons surviving, with a few young girls and a pitiful handful of children to help, and these had to provide food for three days of feasting for a company of one hundred and forty, ninety of them ravenous savages. Fortunately they were spared the task of dishwashing, since there were no utensils except knives to cut up the meat and a few wooden spoons. Forks did not come into general use anywhere in America until the late 1600's. A poem written in 1675 tells us that

". . . the dainty Indian maize
Was eat with clampshells out of wooden trays."

The Pilgrims probably used clamshell spoons and wooden trenchers also.

While the women cooked for the three-day feast, the men indulged in games and exercise of arms. The Indians competed in marksmanship with bows and arrows; red men and white vied in leaping and jumping and racing. There were games of stool ball, in which a ball was batted through wickets, a sort of rough-and-tumble croquet. This favorite sport of the Pilgrim youth was usually frowned on by the Saints, who considered games a frivolous waste of time; on this holiday, however, discipline was relaxed.

Miles Standish marched and countermarched his little band of soldiers, every man except Governor Bradford and Elder Brewster joining the parade. They discharged blank volleys and blew their bugles for the delight and wonder of the savage guests.

These few days of abandonment to worldly pleasures were a wholesome release for the colonists, whose lives had been meager and severe. To share what they had in lavish hospitality with their savage neighbors gave them a sense of well-being, and though they paid for their generosity in bitter deprivation the following winter, they had no regrets.

VI

Other New England Thanksgivings

THERE was no Thanksgiving feast the following autumn; the harvest was too meager to give cause for rejoicing or to permit hospitality. But two years after the first festival—on the 30th of July, 1623—the Pilgrims held a day of Thanksgiving which some authorities hold to be the first real Thanksgiving, since it was the first day that was formally set apart by the governor as a day of prayer. It was not a harvest festival but a public time of thankfulness to the Divine Providence which saved the colony from drought and starvation.

The feeling of security and gratitude which their first fall crops had given the Pilgrims was short-lived. When the harvest festival was over and cold weather was approaching, they "tooke an exacte accounte of all their provisions in store and proportioned the same to the number of persons and found that it would not hold out above six months at half allowance, and hardly that."

There had been great rejoicing when another ship from home was sighted coming into Plymouth harbor, but the enthusiasm cooled when they discovered that the *Fortune* was bringing thirty-five new colonists and no provisions! This meant more hands to work, but also more mouths to be fed from the already meager stores. Their corn was exhausted, except what they had to save for seed, since they could not expect to come upon any further Indian stores. The game that had been so plentiful in the woods and marshes in the autumn disappeared with the coming of winter, as did the eels and herring and lobsters which had been easily caught along the shore and in the streams. There were plenty of fish in the sea, but the colonists had no gear for deep-sea fishing. "In these straits," wrote Winslow, "such was our state as, in the morning we had often our food to seeke for the day and yet performed the duties of our calling. And that at times, in some seasons, at noon I have seen men stagger, by reason of faintness for want of food, yet ere night, by the good providence and blessing of God, we have enjoyed such plenty as though the windows of heaven had opened to us."

In midsummer the white sails of two more ships were sighted in the bay and again the Pilgrims' hopes ran high. These ships were the *Charity* and the *Swan,* bringing sixty men to settle in the colony; but they carried little with them except unpleasant letters from the Pilgrims' backers in England who were disappointed that they had not received valuable cargoes of furs and fish from the colony. This indeed was "cold comforte for hungry bellies."

Among these later arrivals were some highly undesirable characters who stole from the scanty stores of food and stirred up so much trouble with the Indians that Bradford had to send Squanto to Massasoit to explain that these people were "a distincte body from us, and we have nothing to doe with them." Nevertheless, these irresponsible settlers had caused such ill feeling that the Pilgrims had to take precious time from their farming to build a stockade for protection from the savages. Fortunately, they were never attacked. This may have been due partly to the fact that Squanto told the Indians that the Pilgrims kept the plague buried under the Common House in barrels. The barrels really held gunpowder, but since the Indians were much more afraid of the white man's diseases than they were of his "peeces," this proved to be a very effective check on aggression: the first threat of bacteriological warfare, even if an empty one.

The winter of 1623 was a grim one, and in the spring a drought set in which lasted from the third week in May until well into July. The precious crops withered and the colonists were in despair. The Governor appointed a day for fasting and prayer and, after nine hours of supplication to the Deity, clouds moved across the sky from the sea and blotted out the burning sun. By morning a gentle rain was falling, reviving the scorched fields and also the spirits of the colonists. A few days later Captain Standish, who had gone off on a journey to forage for food, returned, bringing not only fresh supplies but the news that the *Anne* was approaching, a ship bearing many of the friends who had been left behind in Leyden when there was not room for them on the *Mayflower*. In view of these blessings, the Governor proclaimed the 30th of July, 1623, as a day of prayer and thanksgiving for the entire colony. As was said above, this may be counted as the first real Thanksgiving Day, since it was the first time that a day was appointed officially by the governor for both religious and social celebration.

On February 22nd, 1630, a day of public thanksgiving was held in Boston by the Bay Colony. This was in celebration of the safe arrival of ships bringing food and friends from Europe.

In 1665, the Court of Connecticut Public Records notes that "This court doth appoint a solemn day of Thanksgiving to be kept throughout this colony on the last Wednesday of October . . . for the blessing of the fruits of the earth and the general health of the plantations."

All these colonial Thanksgivings were regional holidays, and, though they were proclaimed in a religious spirit, family reunion, feasting, and free hospitality were always the spirit of the day. Each colony appointed its own Thanksgiving date, but sometimes the various townships ignored the proclamations and held Thanksgiving at whatever time suited their own convenience. For example, the town of Colchester disregarded the appointed day and held its festival a week later in order to allow time for the arrival of a hogshead of molasses that was due in by sloop from New York. After all, how could they celebrate Thanksgiving without molasses for pumpkin pies and Indian pudding!

A diary kept by Juliana Smith of Massachusetts in 1779 gives an account of an early New England Thanksgiving. This was written as a letter to a cousin, Betsey Smith, but Juliana, not wishing any of her fine phrases to be lost, copied it off in her diary also. One of her descendants, Helen Evertson Smith, discovered the diary and permitted it to be published. The letter reads, in part:

"This year it was Uncle Simeon's turn to have the dinner at his house, but of course we all helped them as they help us when it is our turn, & there is always enough for us all to do. All the baking of pies & cakes was done at our house & we had the big oven heated & filled twice each day for three days before it was all done, & *everything was* GOOD, though we did have to do without some things that ought to be used. Neither Love nor [paper] Money could buy Raisins, but our good red cherries dried without the pits, did almost as well & happily Uncle Simeon still had some spices in store. The tables were set in the Dining Hall and even that big room had no space to spare when we were all seated. The Servants had enough ado to get around the Tables & serve us all without over-setting things. There were our two Grandmothers side by side. They are always handsome old Ladies, but now, many thought, they were handsomer than ever, & happy they were to look around upon so many of their descendants. Uncle & Aunt Simeon presided at one Table, & Father & Mother at the other. Besides us five boys & girls there were two of the Gales & three Elmers, besides James Browne & Ephraim Cowles. [Five of the last-named seven, were orphans taught and in all ways provided for by Parson & Mrs. Smith.] We had them at our table because they could be best *supervised* there. Most of the students had gone to their own homes for the weeks, but Mr. Skiff and Mr. —— [name illegible] were too far away from their homes. They sat at Uncle Simeon's table & so did Uncle Paul and his family, five of them in all, & Cousins Phin & Poll [probably Phineas and Apollos Smith, sons of Dan]. Then there were six of the Livingston family next door. They had never seen a Thanksgiving Dinner before, having been used to keep Christmas Day instead, as is the wont in New York & Province. Then there were four Old Ladies who have no longer Homes or Children of their own & so came to us. They were invited by my Mother, but Uncle and Aunt Simeon wished it so.

"Of course we could have no Roast Beef. None of us have tasted Beef this three years back as it all must go to the Army, & too little they get, poor fellows. But, Nayquittymaw's Hunters were able to get us a fine red Deer, so that we had a good haunch of Venisson on each Table. These were balanced by huge Chines of Roast Pork at the other ends of the Tables. Then there was on one a big Roast Turkey & on the other a Goose, & two big Pigeon Pasties. Then there was an abundance of good Vegetables of all the old Sorts & one which I do not believe you have yet seen. Uncle Simeon had imported the Seede from England just before the War began & only this Year was there enough for Table use. It is called Sellery & you eat it without cooking. It is very good served with meats. Next year Uncle Simeon says he will be able to raise enough to give us all some. It has to be taken up, roots & all & buried in earth in the cellar through the winter & only pulling up some when you want it to use.

"Our Mince Pies were good although we had to use dried Cherries as I told you, & the meat was shoulder of Venisson, instead of Beef. The Pumpkin Pies, Apple Tarts & big Indian Puddings lacked for nothing save *appetite* by the time we had got round to them.

"Of course we had no Wine. Uncle Simeon has still a cask or two, but it must all be saved for the sick, & indeed, for those who are well, good Cider is a sufficient Substitute. There was no Plumb

Pudding, but a boiled Suet Pudding, stirred thick with dried Plumbs & Cherries, was called by the old Name & answered the purpose. All the other spice had been used in the Mince Pies, so for this Pudding we used a jar of West India preserved Ginger which chanced to be left of the last shipment which Uncle Simeon had from there, we chopped the Ginger small and stirred it through with the Plumbs and Cherries. It was *extraordinary* good. The Day was bitter cold & when we got home from Meeting, which Father did not keep over long by reason of the cold, we were glad eno' of the fire in Uncle's Dining Hall, but by the time the dinner was one-half over those of us who were on the fire side of one Table was forced to get up & carry our plates with us around to the far side of the other Table, while those who had sat there were as glad to bring their plates around to the fire side to get warm. All but the Old Ladies who had a screen put behind their chairs.

"Uncle Simeon was in his best mood, and you know how good that is! He kept both Tables in a roar of laughter with his droll stories of the days when he was studying medicine in Edinborough, & afterwards he & Father & Uncle Paul joined in singing Hymns & Ballads. You know how fine their voices go together. Then we all sang a Hymn and afterwards my dear Father led us in prayer, remembering all Absent Friends before the Throne of Grace, & much I wished that my dear Betsey was here as one of us, as she has been of yore.

Bellman reading the Governor's Thanksgiving Proclamation in a New England town (Courtesy of The Bettmann Archive)

Thanksgiving in New York. Young masqueraders demand gifts of promenaders on Fifth Avenue. From a drawing by C. Levi, 1904 (Courtesy of The Bettmann Archive)

Thanksgiving at a New England farmhouse. From a drawing by F. A. Chapman

"We did not rise from the Table until it was quite dark, & then when the dishes had been cleared away we all got round the fire as close as we could, & cracked nuts, & sang songs & told stories. At least some told & others listened. *You know nobody* can exceed the two Grandmothers at telling tales of all the things they have seen themselves, & repeating those of the early years in New England, & even some in the Old England, which they had heard in their youth from their Elders. My Father says it is a goodly custom to hand down all worthy deeds & traditions from Father to Son, as the Israelites were commanded to do about the Passover & as the Indians here have always done, because the Word that is spoken is remembered longer than the one that is written. . . . Brother Jack, who did not reach here until late on Wednesday though he had left College very early on Monday Morning & rode with all due diligence considering the snow, brought an orange to each of the Grandmothers, but Alas! they were frozen in his saddle bags. We soaked the frost out in cold water, but I guess they wasn't as good as they should have been?"

The menus of such old-fashioned dinners cannot but lead the calorie-counting, figure-conscious modern to shudder at the lusty appetites of his forebears! After these collations the older members retired in a glassy-eyed stupor for an after-dinner snooze or a bit of quiet gossip and reminiscence, but for the youngsters there were after-dinner games which were as traditional for Thanksgiving as ducking for apples is for Hallowe'en.

One of these was the Cranberry Contest. The players, each supplied with a large needle and a long coarse thread, stood around a big bowl of raw cranberries. At a given signal all pitched in and threaded as many cranberries as he could in the allotted three minutes. The one who strung the most cranberries won a prize and the privilege of hanging his ruby necklace about the neck of his chosen one with the accompaniment of a hearty kiss.

Another Thanksgiving entertainment was the Corn Game. The properties needed for this game were five ears of dried corn and, of course, a prize for the winner. The five ears of corn were in tribute to the five grains of corn which, legend has it, were the daily ration of the Pilgrims during that second grim winter. The corn was hidden about the house, and the finders were the "finalists" in the game, the other players standing about and cheering while these five vied to see who could strip the cob of its kernels in the shortest time.

The Pumpkin Race was another Thanksgiving sport. The contestants lined up, each with a small pumpkin and a wooden spoon. The prize in this case was awarded to the one who could roll his pumpkin to the finish line first. Since the pumpkin is a lopsided fruit and the contestants could use only the spoon to guide it, the wobbling course provided much hilarity.

A favorite Thanksgiving custom among the youngsters was the practice of dressing in fantastic costume, putting on masks or painting faces, and parading through the streets on Thanksgiving morning begging from passers-by. This mummery started as a re-enactment of the coming of the Indians to the Pilgrim feast. One can still see, on the streets of eastern cities at Thanksgiving, such gangs of oddly costumed children, usually from the poorer classes and of course unaware of the historical background of their prank.

VII

The First National Thanksgiving Proclamation

It WAS not until the thirteen colonies had been united by the Revolution that a general day of Thanksgiving was proclaimed. On September 25th, 1789, Elias Boudinot, member from New Jersey, rose up in the newly formed National Congress and presented a resolution which read: "That a joint committee of both Houses be directed to wait upon the President of the United States, to request that he would recommend to the people of the United States, a day of public Thanksgiving and prayer, to be observed by acknowledging with grateful hearts the many signal favors of Almighty God, especially by affording them an opportunity peaceably to establish a Constitution of government for their safety and happiness."

One would not expect such a resolution to meet with any opposition, but there was vigorous debate on the subject. Ædanus Burke, of South Carolina, objected that this was a mimicking of European customs. Thomas Tucker from the same state protested that the President had no right to demand that the nation offer thanks for a constitution which hadn't been tried out yet and might not be satisfactory. Another felt that this was the business of the states and that the national government should not meddle (a sentiment which has recurred in Congressional argument from that day to this). However, the resolution was finally adopted by both Houses and President Washington issued the First National Thanksgiving Proclamation setting Thursday, November 26th, 1789, as the day. The Proclamation reads as follows:

"Whereas it is the duty of all nations to acknowledge the providence of Almighty God, to obey his will, to be grateful for his benefits, and humbly to implore his protection and favor; and whereas both Houses of Congress have, by their joint Committee, requested me to recommend to the people of the United States a day of Public Thanksgiving and Prayer, to be observed by acknowledging with grateful hearts the many and signal favors of Almighty God, especially by affording them an opportunity peaceably to establish a form of government for their safety and happiness.

"Now therefore I do recommend and assign Thursday, the twenty-sixth of November next, to be devoted by the people of these States to the service of that great and glorious Being, who is the Beneficent Author of all the good that was, that is, or that will be; that we may then all unite in rendering unto him our sincere and humble thanks for his kind care and protection of the people of this country, previous to their becoming a nation; for the signal manifold mercies, and the favorable interpositions of his providence, in the course and conclusion of the late war; for the great degree of tranquillity, union and plenty which we have since enjoyed; for the peaceable and rational manner in which we have been enabled to establish Constitutions of Government for our safety and happiness, and particularly the national one now lately instituted; for the civil and religious liberty with which we are blessed, and the means we have of acquiring and diffusing useful knowledge; and, in general, for all the great and various favors, which he has been pleased to confer upon us.

"And also, that we may then unite in most humbly offering our prayers and supplications to the great Lord and Ruler of Nations, and beseech him to pardon our national and other transgressions; to enable us all, whether in public or private institutions, to perform our several and relative duties properly and punctually; to render our National Government a blessing to all the people, by constantly being a government of wise, just, and constitutional laws, discreetly and faithfully executed and obeyed; to protect and guide all sovereigns and nations (especially such as have shown kindness to us), and to bless them with good governments, peace and concord; to promote the knowledge and practice of true religion and virtue, and the increase of science, among them and us; and, generally, to grant unto all mankind such a degree of temporal prosperity as he alone knows to be best."

VIII

Thanksgiving Becomes
a Legal Holiday

THANKSGIVING did not actually become a national holiday with the Washington Proclamation. Later presidents viewed the custom with indifference, or, as in the case of Thomas Jefferson, with disapproval. Jefferson declared that such proclamations were a "monarchical practice" and ignored this festival during his eight years in office.

John Jay, governor of New York, attempted to establish a statewide Thanksgiving Day in 1795, without much success. The Manhattan Dutch fell in with the idea, but the English on Long Island were in the habit of celebrating Thanksgiving on the first Thursday after the cattle were driven home from the common pastures at Montauk Point. Since this date was a variable one, depending on whether the autumn was a mild or a frosty one, the dairy-men paid no heed to the governor's date. Some of the upstate farmers kept to the old English custom of celebrating whenever the last load of the harvest was stored in the barn. Others, clinging to the Puritan belief that Thanksgiving should be inspired by the beneficence of the Deity rather than the dictates of politicians, ignored the proclamation for religious reasons. Since these groups were unwilling to compromise, Thanksgiving continued to be a regional holiday in spite of the efforts of governors.

However, although the date could not be agreed upon, the Thanksgiving feast had by now become a strong American tradition. Pioneers, seeking new homes in frontier territories, carried the tradition with them and continued to give thanks for the bounty of God in the familiar way. But the pioneers wanted to feel that they were sharing this occasion with the folks back home, saying the same prayers on the same day, gorging on the same foods at the same time. Sentiment was continually growing stronger toward making Thanksgiving an annual holiday on which Americans of all faiths and backgrounds could join in offering thanks to the Creator for their homes in this free and bounteous land.

The most untiring worker toward this goal was Mrs. Sarah Josepha Hale. In *Northwood,* her first novel, written in 1827, she says "Thanksgiving like the Fourth of July should be considered a national festival and observed by all our people." She devotes a whole chapter of this novel to a description of a Thanksgiving dinner with a staggering menu. The roasted turkey "took precedence . . . sending forth the rich odor of its savory stuffing," and "pumpkin pie was an indispensable part of a good and true Yankee Thanksgiving." In 1835 she wrote, with more feeling of social significance, "There is a deep moral influence in these periodical seasons of rejoicing in which whole communities participate. They bring out, and together, as it were, the best sympathies of our nature."

It was not until 1846, however, nine years after she became editor of the famous *Godey's Lady's Book* of Philadelphia, that she launched her full-scale campaign to make Thanksgiving a national holiday. During the seventeen years between this date and the issuing of the Lincoln Proclamation in 1863, Mrs. Hale wrote hundreds of letters to prominent people in all walks of life, urging her cause. Each autumn, *Godey's* carried impassioned editorials on this subject—as well as recipes for toothsome dishes to supplement the turkey: "Indian Pudding with Frumenty sauce"; "ham soaked in cider three weeks, stuffed with sweet potatoes, and baked in maple syrup."

In November 1858, when disunion was already threatening the Republic, Mrs. Hale urged editorially: "If every state would join in Union Thanksgiving on the 24th of this month, would it not be a renewed pledge of love and loyalty to the Constitution of the United States which guarantees peace, prosperity, progress, and perpetuity to our great Republic?"

The next November the nation was torn by civil

strife. In 1861 the lady editor urged that the nation "lay aside our enmities" for one day and join in a Thanksgiving Day of Peace. This plea went unheeded. Though the nation's energies were consumed by the war, Mrs. Hale did not give up her mission. It is highly probably that she paid a personal visit to Abraham Lincoln to put her case before him. In any event, on October 3rd, 1863, in the midst of the Civil War, Lincoln issued a National Thanksgiving Proclamation, the first since that of Washington in 1789.

"The year that is drawing toward its close has been filled with the blessings of fruitful fields and healthful skies. To these bounties, which are so constantly enjoyed that we are prone to forget the source from which they come, others have been added, which are of so extraordinary a nature that they cannot fail to penetrate and soften the heart which is habitually insensible to the ever-watchful providence of almighty God. In the midst of a civil war of unequaled magnitude and severity, which has sometimes seemed to foreign states to invite and provoke their aggressions, peace has been preserved with all nations, order has been maintained, the laws have been respected and obeyed, and harmony has prevailed everywhere, except in the theater of military conflict; while that theater has been greatly contracted by the advancing armies and navies of the Union.

"Needful diversions of wealth and of strength

from the fields of peaceful industry to the national defense have not arrested the plow, the shuttle, or the ship; the ax has enlarged the borders of our settlements, and the mines, as well of iron and coal as of the precious metals, have yielded even more abundantly than heretofore. Population has steadily increased, notwithstanding the waste that has been made in the camp, the siege, and the battlefield, and the country, rejoicing in the consciousness of augmented strength and vigor, is permitted to expect continuance of years with large increase of freedom.

"No human counsel hath devised, nor hath any mortal hand worked out these great things. They are the gracious gifts of the most high God, who, while dealing with us in anger for our sins, hath nevertheless remembered mercy.

"It has seemed to me fit and proper that they should be solemnly, reverently, and gratefully acknowledged as with one heart and one voice by the whole American people. I do, therefore, invite my fellow-citizens in every part of the United States, and also those who are at sea and those who are sojourning in foreign lands, to set apart and observe the last Thursday of November next as a day of thanksgiving and praise to our beneficent Father who dwelleth in the heavens. And I recommend to them that, while offering up the ascriptions justly due to him for such singular deliverances and blessings, they do also, with humble penitence for our national perverseness and dis-

93

obedience, commend to his tender care all those who have become widows, orphans, mourners, or sufferers in the lamentable civil strife in which we are unavoidably engaged, and fervently implore the interposition of the almighty hand to heal the wounds of the nation, and to restore it, as soon as may be consistent with the Divine purposes, to the full enjoyment of peace, harmony, tranquillity, and union."

With the Lincoln Proclamation Thanksgiving became a legal holiday on which the whole nation closes its shops, offices, schools, and banks, and offers its thanks to the Deity for the blessings of this free and bountiful land. Although, officially, the date is set each year by presidential proclamation, the fourth Thursday of November became the traditional Thanksgiving Day. Great was the consternation, therefore, when in 1939 Franklin Delano Roosevelt, that famous breaker of precedents, proclaimed November 23rd, the *third* Thursday, as Thanksgiving. The reason for the change was that the merchants had complained that the interval between Thanksgiving and Christmas was so short that they could not make proper provision for the December holiday rush.

Although this seemed a sensible adjustment, there were loud protesting outcries in the land. Irate Republicans appealed to the Pilgrim Fathers, the Founding Fathers, and even the Constitution. Football coaches, whose schedules for the all-important Thanksgiving Day games had been arranged on the assumption that November 30th was the Day, groaned and cursed That Man in the White House. The country was divided into two camps: those who accepted the proclamation and feasted on the 23rd, and those who held to the traditions of their forefathers and dined on the 30th. Harassed mothers didn't know when to cook the turkey, for some of the children had their holiday on the 23rd and some on the 30th. After two years of this confusion, Thanksgiving went back to the fourth Thursday, and it is doubtful that any future president will flout tradition again by changing the date.

We have come a long way in a short book; from the Eleusinian Mysteries of the ancient Greeks to the eccentricities of the New Deal. But this wide span merely goes to show that human nature has not changed greatly over the centuries. The emotional need to express gratitude to the Deity for the bounty of the earth is ages old, as is likewise the joy of human beings in coming together for feasting and sharing this bounty with those they hold dear.

'The story of Thanksgiving would not be complete without the inclusion of that merry jingle written nearly a hundred years ago by Lydia Maria Child. Although the modern child does not go to Grandmother's by sleigh—indeed there is rarely any snow on Thanksgiving nowadays,

even in the northern states—this old song still
echoes from every schoolroom in America as November brings happy expectations of the Thanksgiving feast:

> Over the river and through the wood,
>   To grandfather's house we go;
>   The horse knows the way
>   To carry the sleigh
>   Through the white and drifted snow.
>
> Over the river and through the wood—
>   Oh, how the wind does blow!
>   It stings the toes
>   And bites the nose,
>   As over the ground we go.
>
> Over the river and through the wood,
>   To have a first-rate play.
>   Hear the bells ring.
>   "Ting-aling-ding!"
>   Hurrah for Thanksgiving Day!
>
> Over the river and through the wood
>   Trot fast, my dapple-gray!
>   Spring over the ground
>   Like a hunting hound,
>   For this is Thanksgiving Day.
>
> Over the river and through the wood,
>   And straight through the barn-yard gate.
>   We seem to go
>   Extremely slow—
>   It is so hard to wait.

The Story of Thanksgiving

Over the river and through the wood—
  Now grandmother's cap I spy!
    Hurrah for the fun!
    Is the pudding done?
  Hurrah for the pumpkin pie!

Index

Index